beneath the surface

beneath the surface

A BOOK OF POEMS

BARBARA GARAY

BENEATH THE SURFACE © 2019 Barbara Garay

All rights reserved.

ISBN: 978-0-578-45866-3

THIS BOOK IS DEDICATED TO

To my son and my daughter. My heart overflows with love for them everyday.
To my husband for always showing me unconditional love.
To my adopted mother, Katarzyna Jasiula, who no longer is with us. She taught me to love and forgive when I thought I no longer could.
To Cari "Rage" Bermudez for being a huge inspiration to me.

CONTENTS

Acknowledgments viii

Preface x

Roots 1

Love 15

Heartbreak 47

Inner Struggles 67

Resilience 89

ACKNOWLEDGMENTS

The following have my deepest thanks: Michelle Whiting who is like a mother to me; Sugar Blue who is like a father to me; my family; my editor Jen Chichester; and Jamileth Reyes for allowing me to take photos of her for the cover of this book.

PREFACE

The poem is a snapshot of a moment frozen in time. It is packed with an emotive power that brings to life a theme or event most of us have experienced at some point in our lives. Therefore, the poem is much more than just words. The poem is a bridge that connects the reader to an emotional journey.

This book explores the experience of enduring trauma, the struggle of finding love and connection, and the battle with depression/anxiety. It attempts to illustrate that pain eventually leads to a type of strengthening. We endure, we learn, we rise, and we evolve. We are in a perpetual bloom as we strive to rise above ground while still tethered to the roots of our past.

The poets that have inspired me in my writing journey include Rumi, Yeats, Rainer Maria Rilke, and Edgar Allan Poe. Their words reveal the way in which poetry is a means to dig deep into our inwardness in order to cultivate a higher level of awareness about our inner self and our role in the world. Therefore, poetry taps into the depths of our human psyche by unmasking our vulnerabilities, our pain, our past, our weaknesses, our strengths, and our footprints thus far in the world. In this way, it becomes one of the most honest means of self-expression and an immediate tool for healing.

Additionally, philosophy has always been a great source of inspiration for me. It fuels my hunger for knowledge and translates into my writing. Some of the thinkers that have highly influenced my life include Friedrich Nietzsche, Soren Kierkeegard, Simone de Beauvoir, and most importantly, Emmanuel Levinas. This list is by no means exhaustive, but the words of these particular thinkers in many ways have become a part of me and my poetry.

I now implore you to venture into the words that bare my soul as I unravel my traumatic past, my adventures with love and heartbreak, and my inner battles. Join me in my journey to find meaning in this world as I heal and forgive all the roots that are tethered to this mind and body. It is my hope that you may feel less alone in your own experience of similar events as you read my poetry. It is also my hope that you may find inspiration to heal, forgive, find meaning, and rise as well.

Barbara Garay

1 ROOTS

Branches of the past
entwine with our web-shaped veins,
and we trace each line until we find
the secret of who we are
buried within
deepest rooted memories.

Uprooted

My feet
plucked from soil
while very young
learned the meaning
of a soul at home
when I lost my own.
To my mother I clung
as the plane rose higher
into a non-world
where I'd fight
to be a survivor.
My somber heart
buried itself into my
inward part
as I became
a stranger in a
world unknown,
a stranger
without a home.
It is here wounds began
to form
for I wouldn't see
a permanent home
until I've grown.

Flesh

Home is in the skin
sheltering a soul,
pieces of selves
stored on our shelves
as skin holds together
nerves, muscles, bones,
and our identities
become shaped
by the folds in our
fleshly cobblestones.
Walls enclose our
v u l n e r a b i l i t y ;
displacement exposes
our skin's fragility.

Daydreamer

As a child,
my mind
was a warm
place of refuge,
a hiding place
within a deluge
of imaginings;
a secret sanctuary
when all was
tumultuary.

                        In hard times,
                        I still go there.

Sky Watcher

Sky watcher
and star gazer
epitomize
who I was
as a child.
My eyes
would absorb
colors from clouds
and use every
tint of blue
to wipe away
the dirt from
my life,
turning tears
into aquamarine gems
with a shade of blue
that was brighter
than the blue found
in all of space.
It is here
I grew the desire
to spread my soul
across the sky
like a raging wildfire.

Angel

Thinking back to
when I was nine,
and the saturation
of my blood
had a tint of youth
with a flood of hope
pouring from my eye,
I imagined I would
one day fly
with angels in the sky.
As I became older,
my soul grew deeper,
my heart grew sadder,
and those angels
m e t a m o r p h o s e d
into ideals disclosed
within the human eye
or diminished
with every spoken lie.

Between

Even as a child,
I'd always fade
into a place
existing
between my dreams
lulling me
from above
and reality
pulling my feet
from below.

Only now,
this tension
keeps me
grounded.

Breaking the Cycle

My real mother
never exhaled
"I love you"
into my ear.
But I know
the world
never bathed her
in love either.

It is a cycle,
but I think
the cycle breaks
when one
forgives the other.

And so,
I forgave
my mother
and exhaled
"I love you"
into her ear
as I cared
and comforted her
before
death took her.

Devil Disguised in Flesh

I remember
when my mother
came home
with an open skull,
blood dripped
down her face.
Her eyes
full of tears,
her heart
full of fears.
She told me
it was the man
that lived next door,
but I thought
it was the devil
in the air,
the devil disguised
in flesh and hair.
How else
could a child
understand
a man
hitting a woman
in the head
with a chair?

Repressed Memories

I still hear the storm
ambush my mind
with rain punching glass,
the pitter and the patter
s y n c h r o n i z i n g
with the drum
inside my chest.
I still see
the flashing image
of little legs
crawling out of bed
and taking shelter
on the floor
with a blanket over head,
and it reminds me
of all the cold nights
I spent alone as a child,
with a monster
next door,
with a monster
next door.

Masked Bruises

It felt unfortunate
being born
on days when the gentle
summer breeze
would caress my skin
and lift the thin fabric of my
yellow summer dress,
revealing bruises
all-over-skin.

How quick they would gaze
and make the dirt inside
begin to grow,
reminding me,
reminding me,
reminding me.

Abuse

Dark annihilates light,
little girl's chest
fills with fright
each night
the monster scowls,
whipping the child
with its growl.
She hides
inside her mind
and prays for a hand
that's kind,
but continual silence
disturbs the balance
and releases
bitter tasting betrayal
l a d e n
with ashen waste
that is still felt
inside her mouth
this-very-day.

Blue

I hold roots
inside my palm,
they puncture skin
and release
blue blood
all over me,
revealing wounds
of being born
into a world
deeply forlorn,
my branches grow
razor-tipped edges
cutting deep,
forcing me to see
bruised-up blue
instead of beautiful.
Despite it all,
I still hold
so much love
inside of me.

2 LOVE

Tethered to the light
of the other,
I give up love
with effortless grace,
silky soft,
like layered latticed lace,
and with reckless abandon,
passionately poetic,
I set fire to every tendon.

Sacred Alterity, Ode to Levinas

Your face speaks
when you hold
my gaze.
Infinity flows
from your eyes
like waves
rolling up to the shore.
Paralyzed and unable
to move past the sand,
I am prohibited
from delineating
the shape of your soul
by my hand,
for your alterity is yours
and cannot be defined,
it is not a thing
to own or call mine.

Friendship

I'll gather your tears
in the same way
a petal catches a dewdrop.
I'll catch your dreams
in the same way
glass catches sunbeams.
I'll encourage that smile,
go the extra mile,
and be the bone
in your back
to help you stand
when you feel like
you are going to crack.
I'll fill the empty space
that lingers
by pouring
a piece of my soul
onto your fingers.

Pale White Hand

I wrap my heart
in layered love,
and set it adrift
within the sea
of memory
where you reside
beyond all time,
and you are held
by all that is sublime.

Burn

Your love
makes me curl
like a soft petal
on a hot summer day.
My guard
is down.
Let your flame
burn me
as it drips
down my vein.

Desire

The ravenous itch
caresses the lining
of my veins
and listens to the song
that my heart emits
endearing the itch
of longing
to slither into my cells.

                    This is what
                    you do to me.

                    Everyday.

Flame

Your beauty scorches me
like a flame kissing skin,
a w a k e n i n g
an unrelenting sea
buried deep within.

Drifters

We are unknowns
lost in all this
empty space
and fleeting time.
Sentimental stirrings
transform into yearnings
as we collapse
into each other's eyes,
dissecting every atom
while moving through
the soul's stratum
in search
of something
we can't
ever fathom.

Eternal

There is something
in the way the sun
drenches you
in golden hues,
making you appear
imperishable and true,
eternal too,
as if your bones
are made of holy gold
and my heart
is yours to mold.

A Fateful Encounter

Our paths crossed
in August
amidst an unrelenting heat.
I wore my broken trust,
yet he still managed
to catch my lust.
But see, we were always
meant to be,
this encounter designed
as if the stars purposely aligned
to ensure that miles away from home
two soulmates would roam,
two soulmates would find
their forever home
inside each other,
as if guided by
a predetermined endeavor.

Our Home

I meander
through the space
that fills our halls
and press my ears
against cold walls
to hear
the steady pulse
our love transmits
within this home,
within *our* home.
Our home is my only
place of refuge,
for the only place
I want to encase
my soul in
is inside
the space that hums
our life into my ear.

Beyond Love

We threw our hearts
into the sky
and painted clouds
a faded shade of red
like the rising
of the sun
in the early dawn.
You took my hand,
and held my gaze,
our bodies saturated
by colors swirling
in our eyes.
We learned that love
does not fade with time,
instead, it transforms
into a strong
celestial dome
called home.

Crave

The nebulous untrodden road
inside of your eyes
winds itself
into my bleeding heart.
You take my breath away,
and suspend all movement of time,
my soul becomes your clay
that you shape into
what it means
for me to be alive.

Flash

That piercing flash
from your eye
and the warm
curved line
formed by your lips
is a gentle song
that speaks to me
and takes my mind
on a creative stroll.

And so I write
and I write
until you fill
every page,
and become
every poem.

Emerald Seas

Emerald seas
flood your eyes
and pour into me,
you wrap me in a sigh
that you exhale
like a warm and gentle
summer breeze.
You free my mind
and calm my wild
with the magic
burrowed in your eye.

Temptation

Her delicate face
wrapped in ivory and lace
hides behind rose leaves
as temptation drips
from her sleeves.

Allure slips from her lips
and the sway of her hips
lures me in to take
infinitesimal sips.

I falter in my step,
undoing everything I've kept,
and my fatality is put to rest
while my ethics face
an enduring test.

Oh, but how that allure
slips from her lips
and the sway of her hips
lures me in to take
those infinitesimal sips.
She makes it hard
n o t t o s l i p .

Galaxy Eyes

When I gaze
into your eyes,
I am beholden
by a cluster
of stars.
They pull
the gravity
out from
beneath my feet,
and make me fall
into the realm
where reality
and fantasy meet.

Droplets

I remember
when you
transmuted my soul
into water,
your palm
cradled my droplets
with solicitude
as you held them up
toward the sun
so they would dry
into your skin.

Gentle Touch

The softness
in your touch
laces me with sin
as if silk
is woven
into your skin.
Heavy chains
holding
my sunken remains
lighten
from each embrace,
reversing
the somber
on my face,
and love begins
to occupy this space.

Fall & Fade

I fall and fade into
the rhythmic serenade
s i n g i n g
inside your chest.
It gives me rest.
Our inwardness
begins to coalesce
and forms
transcendent love.
With each caress,
I e m e r g e
an exultant dove
within this love.

Skin Deep

He proclaims
as he takes
a glimpse
beneath my flesh
that my beauty
is skin deep,
and plunging
into my eyes
is like jumping into
an ocean
with no floor.
Maybe he can find
my lost soul
in all the vastness
he explores.

Rainy Days

When rain falls
it fills my heart
with dreary and dark.
Life can be so cold
without a spark.
Then you come along,
the sun blazing
in your smile,
every breath so warm,
it melts away
the cold.
You are a flood
of light,
you are the day
to my night.

Esoteric Mind

Your esoteric mind
entwines deeply
with mine
and here we are
swimming
in the unraveling
as our souls align.

Allure

A rhythm pulsates
from beneath
your pores.
It reels me in,
I succumb,
and become yours.
When you speak,
I sink
with every motion
of your lip,
your voice becomes
the ink
forcing
my secrets
to slip.

Atoms

Two atoms entangled,
you and I,
possessed by a love
that cannot be dismantled.
Our energies, when combined,
will resist the atrophic
erosion of flesh
forthcoming in humankind,
and when the stars
burn out,
we will occupy all space
with our timeless glow
and illuminate the darkened skies
with the love in our eyes.

Jasmine

Her strong sillage
of Jasmine
diffuses
in the air
and leaves me
ashen
when the sweet
elusive trail
fades
with each inhale.

Scent is
as powerful
as presence,
and lingers
in absence.

Gifting Compassion

Please do not
gift me
diamonds
laced
with blood.
Please do not
gift me daisies
that will sit and rot.
It is your
compassion
that I want.

I Wait

I wait for you
to loosen the strings
that fine-tune my being
and thread love
into my sinew
while I fade into you.

I wait for you
to pluck my strings
and play them like a lyre
awakening my inner muse
to emerge from the fire.

I wait for you
to trace the antiquity
tucked away in my mind
and disclose the possibilities
you unearth from my bind.

Holding Hands

A graceful endeavor
hand in hand
for now and forever
toward unknown lands.
We both go in blind,
that's the best kind
living through fingers
causing sensation
to linger.

Open Roads

Your chestnut eyes
disclose open roads
inside your soul
inviting me
to take a ride
right by your side.
You reach
beneath my skin
and unpin
the veil
to expose each detail
of my scars.
You turn them
into stars
as you untwine the vine
coiled tight
around my heart.

Best Friend

She knocked on the door
that led to my being,
I allowed her to see
the gaping hole
across my collar bone,
her eyes grew warm
and light began to swarm,
with a shovel in her hand,
and dirt in the other,
she dived into my wonderland
to make me whole again,
to make me love again,
to make me warm again.

3 HEARTBREAK

You-are-not-mine;
the words sink
and soak the collagen
inside my bone.

Crushed Clover

Smashed clover
within my palm,
luck will not
bring you home.
Time, a cruel fate
to memory
prompts me
to embalm ours
t e n d e r l y
and slow down
the imminent decay
of the days
before you went away,
of times we sat
beneath the stars
measuring
the depth of our scars,
ruminating
on our immanence
while losing our innocence.

A Stroll

You ventured on
a hermeneutic stroll
into
the darkest layer
of my soul,
convinced me
of its beauty
until you let it go,
leaving nothing more
but a fading echo.

Muse

My muse is a force
that overwhelms me
to the ground
and absorbs my soul
with a tranquil sound.
Tethered to this other
by a longing unsurrendered,
my soul is bared to suffer
as a profuse void is rendered.

Turquoise Sea

I feel you
inside the wind
lightly grazing
at my skin.
I carry you
inside of me
and pour
these memories
over me
that turn you
into
my turquoise sea.

Conquest

You caress my face
with the razor in your voice,
masked with silken kisses,
designed to bring me
to the floor.
You claim my skin
as your noble win,
an object for you to hold,
an object for you to mold.
But I won't let you
near my soul,
that's **mine,**
and there
you will never go.

Power

The pain you cause
vibrates into my skin
i n v o k i n g
an earthquake within,
it wears me down so thin
as shockwaves infiltrate
the nerves
and rattle up my bones
until my foundation
crumbles to a pile of stones.

Pivot

The weight of this love,
suspended from a pivot,
swings toward the warmth
held by her spirit,
time passes,
it oscillates back
to the ice in her eye.
This game, an interplay –
of an invitation to feel
heightened elation
to feeling the grip
of the noose
remove that elation
by strangulation.

Cavernous Eyes

How was I to foretell
the knife to my heart
when into your eyes I fell
unable to find my way out.

Moonglade

You materialize into
a translucent silhouette
followed by
a trail of regret
gliding across
the Moonglade
until the moon sets
dissolving you
into darkness,
leaving me
in blackness.
Alone, I navigate
the sea of loose moments
and endeavor
to drown their contents,
but I am drenched
in so much loneliness
and am unable to
suppress our memories.

Mirage

Pieces of you
cascade into
my mind's view
forming an image
of you
hovering over me
like a mirage I can't
seem to let go.
I starve in
this illusory oasis
that holds me
in perpetual stasis.

Crooked Smile

I mistook
that crooked line
for a sunny smile,
but your mind changes
with the seasons
and I no longer have
a revolving heart.

Spineless

You dug
your sharpened claws
into the ligaments
securing bones
inside my back.
Your deepened grip
ripped them out,
and played me
like an instrument.

She Loves Me, She Loves Me Not

We were ride or die,
you and I, forever friends
until the end
she'd always swear
as she plucked a daisy
and pressed it firmly
into my hair.
But years passed,
and here I am, plucking
each pale white petal
by myself
to make that memory last.
Her absence sears
into my skin,
yet I still whisper,
"she loves me, she loves me not"
into cold air
as I breathe her silence in.

Siren

It seems like
a siren lurks within
the space you used to roam,
her stone-like gaze
strikes me down,
while her song
attuned to a wretched
yet seductive tone,
halts my will
to let you go,
drowning me
so far down
while weaving
my flesh back
into every bit of
desire
that has your name engraved
w i t h i n
the deepest fiber.

Springs

Feelings with you
are fleeting
like ephemeral spirits
dancing
in the midnight sky.
My worth rises
to a feather-light high,
then falls
when you weigh it down
by the anchor you apply.
One moment,
I'm plunging
into the depth
of your eye,
then another,
I'm recoiling like
the spring inside
the barrel of a gun,
absorbing the shock
of your goodbye.
Truth is,
I still feel your silence
pinned to my bone
each time a cold
gust of wind is blown.

Salt

I taste the salt
dripping toward my lip,
your heart a stone vault
I can't seem to grip.

My eyes betray
how much I crave
to have you for another day,
but I am just another wave.

And like a wave,
you'll let me pass you by,
a trace of me you save
in memory behind your eye.

Silent Meadows

How I wish I could say
let's rendezvous at the grove,
leave our troubles at bay
as we ride on our love.
You bring the pearl
to strengthen this bond,
I'll bring the lace
to add grace to the ground.
But you are just a shadow
that weighs on my heart,
and I'm lost in a meadow
where silence keeps us apart.

Midnight Strolls

My mind is strewn
with memories of the way
your chest rose
with the moon
while the ocean waves
played a lullaby
and our energies
were powered by
the catalysts
from our eye to eye.
Your skin embraced
by flecks of sand,
my hand ran a finger
through your silken hair,
until one day
you vanished
into air.

4 INNER STRUGGLES

Finding light amidst
the fogbound dark
can be
a long and fiendish fight,
and in these moments
of despair,
you hear the darkness
whisper
as it gently
strokes your hair.

Absence

Absence colors
my blood to
black,
and fills me
with despair
and lack.
This cursed
ink latches on
to every tick
of my finite time.
I immortalize it
with my rhyme.

One Second Too Late

Nails dig into my flesh,
body paralysis
settles in,
time stands still,
and the first sign
of heaviness
begins to weigh in.
I observe humans
connect as they move
into intricate
social nets,
and I wonder
is there any space
in there
for me?

But I am always
one second
too late,
there is never
any space
l e f t .

Defense Mechanisms

We water seeds we
buried beneath skin
with tears that beget us
to be caged and unfree.
Protectively, we bind
our shells
with silver tin
to cover the delicate within
and hope to smell
our defiant blooms
that will one day
break free from all
that keeps us unfree.

Poets

Poets imbue
words with life
to create the illusion
of a blissful song
to haul
the weighty anguish
cutting through us
like a knife.
We disguise
unadulterated despair
with prose and beauty
of a soul exposed
as fully bare.

Poetry

Peel apart my skin.
Unveil the eloquence
within,
cell and tissue,
the blank paper,
my soul,
the painter,
blood,
the ink
inscribing poetry
while I sink.

My Rhythm

My words
are synchronous
with the rhythm
of my heart.
You can witness
the accent
of my being
as my words
peel apart
feelings
woven into each
syllable
in the same way
a violin
peels apart
melancholy
woven into
its sound,
rendering emotion
v i s i b l e
to the eye.

Heart

Crack open my chest
to find my heart pump
a wounded soul
into my lungs,
which I expel by
breathing out
the words
that make me whole,
then listen to the
rhythm of the beat
as each muscle contracts
around the pain
that I transform
into a rain of poetry.

Grief

Memory of her
extends across time,
blurring the distance
of this timeline.
My limbs move toward
the place of not-here
to a time of not-now,
plunging me into
thick timeless silence
where I propel myself
against layers
of heavy blackness.
I fight to reclaim you from
eternal oblivion,
scream your name,
irradiate your being
with a bright flame,
and draw the contour
of your vein
with a bloodstain
before the darkness
begins to pour you
into a place where
remembrance is no more.

Garden

She grew a garden with her tears,
   traced the petals with the colors in her veins,
     and allowed herself to rise after the passing of a few more years.

       Time does not heal, but it dims all that
       pains by fading out the memories
         we retain.

Secrets

Dormant, they grow inside,
covered by the haze
inside our eyes,
our secrets stray for miles,
creating ripples
in the strings that hold our hearts.
We tug and push them aside
until they manifest
into demons that rip
our souls apart
and make us unkind.
Piece by piece, we break
until our secrets
are released.

Depression

Your jagged edges
catch my eye,
faded and slightly jaded,
are you like me inside?
Does the blackened beast
widen your lungs
each time you breathe?
Does it pull you down
into the ground?
Does the beast envelope you
with arms that surround,
empties blood from veins
and replaces it with weights
that push you down
to kiss cement?
Then, the black pulls
your body into itself,
blue pours from eyes
and flows into the empty space
that beats inside,
leaving you gasping
until the weights are lifted
for a little while.
Eventually, the next wave comes,
but as time goes by,
we learn to sink with grace
and wait the storm out
with a silent stoic face.

Vulnerability

This life
has me
wearing barbed
wire around
my bleeding
heart while
sculpting
vulnerability
into a ceramic
piece of art.

Corridor

I rummaged through
the darkest corridors
of this world to bask
within your light,
intrigued by your
ambiguous existence
shining against
the backdrop
of everything cruel,
the slits of your eyes
came through
like a half-moon
and I knew,
I knew,
you would save me too.

Sinking

I sink into a squat
atop the crunch of
browned and dying leaves,
alone, I claim this spot
and question my beliefs.
Anxiety wounds my chest
as the question
replays inside my head,
"Maybe its me."
In pours
the insidious dread
like the incoming wave of the sea.
I know I carry scars,
and live inside my head,
is this why people seem to flee?

Decadence of Dreams

Dreams decompose
with the passing of time
filling our veins with
reddish-orange rust,
the fires in our hearts
turn to dust,
but their absence lingers
wailing within a mist
that follows
like the translucent swirl
of a ghastly shadow.
We are left with
silver tears upon
our cheeks
and out of our mouths
come wretched shrieks.

Dread

The soul begins
to feel astray
as dread unfolds
dimming the light
to a faded grey,
the pain begins
to make
the heart its prey,
while the body
sails aimlessly
upon this wave,
w a i t i n g
for it to fade.

A Writer's Mind

A writer's mind
at first is a cold
and dreary place
filled with an echo
bouncing off of
empty walls,
where a sea of anxiety
savagely roars from all
the crumpled papers
across the floor
we refuse
to throw away.
See, we can't be sure
if we want to
bring the words
we thought were trash
back to life once more
after we finish fencing
with self-doubt,
or come alive
at the sight
of a human eye.

Bottled Scars

My mind
lightly floats
amongst
thoughts that
appear and fade
like stars.
My body,
weighed down,
carries scars
in small jars.

Chicago Homeless Girl

I used to pass you every day,
at first, you caught my eye
with your smile,
there was light
in your turquoise eye,
a book in your hand, I thought
there's hope for you yet,
until I saw track marks
with blood still wet,
with your life
you play roulette.
And yet, you taught me
how powerful
absence can be felt
during the long interval
when you were
no longer there.
I bet you thought
no one felt yours,
but I-felt-it,
and years later,
I-still-feel-it.

Melancholy

This moment
of weakness
spreads inside
as if a balloon
expands against
my lungs,
and then it bursts,
and I can breathe again,
and I am strong again.

5 RESILIENCE

And so, I forgive the past
and rise into a sky
that requires iron wings to fly,
and if a wasteland blooms inside of me,
then I will be its baroness
controlling what it does to me.

Wandering Soul

I wander to get lost
amidst the wild wilderness
spanning across my mind
where dreams spill into rivers
and memories are bridges
waiting to be crossed.
It is here I commune
with the sweetly surreal
and amass bits of myself
with pensive parturient eyes
preparing to birth strength
into my spine,
prompting me
to heal,
prompting me
to rise.

Living With Memories

We are bound
to memories,
to a past,
even to those full
of all that is aghast,
and yet, we must
conjure up
enough strength
to live beside
our ghosts,
u n a f r a i d.

Solitude

I wear solitude
like my favorite
pair of sweats,
comfortable and free
from life's constraints.
Alone, I reconstitute
my soul
as the world melts away.
It is here that I can hear
the faint whisper
of my voice.
It unveils
the meaning to my being,
this feeling,
of heaviness lifting,
my mind is drifting,
the moon gently
tugs upon my bone
to awaken the universe within
that is yet unknown.
With my hand I trace
the world within my vein
and recollect
scattered fragments
through the recollection
of my pain.

Death

We grow pale
as we face
the direction
of our numbered days.
We feel them
hovering over us
like hawks,
reminding us to face
our mortal limitations,
reminding us
to live and affirm our lives.

Traumatic Memories

Traumatic memories
always come
in overpowering flashes.
When they do,
summon your strength
and focus in
on every breath.
Remember that
the past is the past,
it already passed,
but you live
and you must
keep-treading-on.

Ashes

Dreams weave
themselves
into our minds
like vines,
some of us
let them turn
to ash,
while others,
chase them
all the way
into the sky.

Sonder

Overcome by a moment
of sonder,
deep-set lines
on your face
make me fonder
of their testament
to your human history
shrouded in mystery.
I yearn to fall
into your soul
with a telescopic view
giving access to
the depth in you,
and deconstruct
every atom
as a way of
shortening this chasm
so you no longer manifest
as a type of phantom.
But that would be treason
to your sanctum,
for the space that
holds your infinity
is holy and to define it
would be pure indignity.

Wild Heart

The breeze tugs on her vein
waking the wild within
that society cannot tame
the way they do her skin, but herein
she bares her soul, empowered and free
as the wild cauterizes the wounds
that once bled like the sea,
her spirit becomes attuned
to the parts that set her free.

Cherry Blossom Tree

Her eyes became sealed
beneath cherry blossoms
with the secret she bequeathed
as she exhaled
her final breath.
A rain of pink haze
from above that I embraced
with anger and love
began to fall and dissipate,
alas, the dream began to pass.
My pores began to sweat
a transient gleam,
e x p o s i n g
the fragile temporal seam
sown into the fabric of bone,
e x p o s i n g
an evanescent being that must atone
as death becomes the horizon
that brightens the fullness
of existence.

When her eyes became sealed beneath
cherry blossoms, the secret she bequeathed
was the meaning of death
as she exhaled her final breath.

Nefarious Sea

Waves heighten and tickle
my ribcage as they trickle
down into the hole
pressing upon my being.
Lungs compress
as I am possessed
by the nefarious sea
growing turbulent
inside of me.
I collapse into a barren
void while my sight
begins to darken
from the emptiness
consorting with
the nothingness
that is burning
in my throat.

***Stop* and *breathe*.**

I have been through this
enough times
to know
that this too will pass, and I
inscribe each time I rise
into warm bedazzled brass.

Alpenglow

We start off as saplings
grappling with hardships,
attempting to circumvent
rather than welcoming ascent
as we face life's perplexities
not yet embracing complexities.
Then we grow and expand
as we enter new lands
and question our hands.
It is here we start
scaling walls of history,
and washing away ideology.
The effervescent glow
pours insight
into our marrow
as we stand on mountains,
drinking wisdom from
crystal clear fountains,
basking in the rosy Alpenglow
as we listen to our heart's
penetrating adagio.

Facing Fatality

She proved to be
far from guileless
as she ambushed
my dream and
moved secretly along
the seam that holds
together my being.
Like a ghostly
presence,
she crept around
my essence,
and tormented
my subconscious
while sleep
kept me silenced.
She carved
a line
into a filament
so I could feel her
on my spine
and be reminded
of my finite time.
But, I'm not ready
to make my bed,
so I told her
to get out of my head.

Inner Peace

I find peace
when I dissolve
into waves of
unmitigated silence,
the type of quiet
that lives beneath
the water's violence.
Here, the steady
vibration of
my pulse
makes me whole.

Beneath the Veil

The roles we play
mask the truth
of what may lay
behind our eyes
that when unwove
disclose the secret
of our soul.
We remain
unknown
beneath the veil,
our secret sewn
into a dark abyss
that dims
every sacred detail.

Singularity

You carry
the unknown
within you,
unscripted,
hidden,
from them
and from you,
an enigma
that paints
the inside
of you.

Journey into Myself

Some days
my body
drifts above the surface
dragging without purpose
all the empty I embody.
On these days,
I search for the
glow of a cipher
to guide me to a place
inside me
where I can trace
every enigma
and futilely
attempt to decipher.

Closure in Goodbye

The remnant
of her shadow
burns into my mind.
I am thankful
that at least
I was able to say
goodbye.

Mankind

Perhaps it is mankind
that ought to be
c o n f i n e d
to crouch in the devil's corner
from the way we devise
so much terror.
We carry in us
a heavy bag of darkness
that we unleash
as we oppress
with violence the face
that we try to efface.
The demon rage stains
as it lurks inside our veins,
making it hard to be human
as we sink into ruin.

Tick Tock

We can say
there is no time,
yet here it is,
accumulating
in the folds of our skin,
line after line,
annotating our history
and our decline.

Rusted Veins

Painful memories pour
into our rusted veins
from which we wrap
elaborate heavy chains.
We erect lofty empty walls
to protect the delicate
inside our heart by staying desolate
within these lonely halls.
We sew the chambers
of our heart with a thorn,
and alone we mourn,
bleeding tears into
these dying embers.

But, my love, what if we're ready
to lift the heavy chain
and let them
see beyond the veil again?
Here's my hand to keep you steady.

Will you take it?

My Becoming

Never mistake
my fragility
for weakness,
my innate overcoming
is an ability
that leads to
my becoming.
I allow
these metamorphoses
to bleed out
through my wounds,
then bathe
my soul
in new profound
interior plenitudes.

Fragile Girl

Fragile girl
on the ground of stones,
a cocoon unfurls
a damaged pile of bones.

The cocoon you built
to protect your skin
molded by tears spilt
c r a c k s
to let the metamorphosis begin.

Bones harden
as shields soften, you no longer cry
as you muster a garden
where you emerge a butterfly.

Depth

Depth inks itself into the pages
of a soul that rises strengthened.
Pain throughout the ages
unfolds in layers
of a journey transcended.

Seaborne

My seaborne soul
wanders off to be free
following the wind's flow
over stagnant trees.
It grows robust
from the sea in my vein
and decays if reduced
a slave to the mundane.

Resilience

Even when life
seemed to be
a collection of
surrenders and
goodbyes, I refused
to give up
wearing resilience
as my
armored way of life.
See, hope never
caressed me
or blessed me,
since birth, hope
was never
to be mine.
It was always a
"how much can you endure"
before your bones
come undone.
It was resilient skin
molded from tears
that ripened my heart.

But I always survived.
And I will always survive.

Deep Thinkers

We that tend
to contemplate
the shape of our souls
feel the light of the moon
flow into our veins,
our hearts grow
until they explode
and spread
burning shards
across the night sky
for awhile
until we implode
back into ourselves
and fall like raindrops
to the oceans below.

Overcoming the Past

Don't let demons
of your past clip
the wings
to your future.
Face them,
understand them,
conquer them.
Let them become
the wind
that will guide
the unfolding
that is burgeoning
in your soul
to soar.

Accepting Temporality

In time,
everyone fades away,
transfiguring into
echoes that latch
onto our memories
and bleed our hearts dry.

Comatized

The unconscious colossus
of the algorithm
behind the coded word, at first,
aimed to bring us together
now quickly tears apart
the connecting tether.
When was the last time
you gazed upward
toward the infinity
carrying the sky,
or the last time
you prioritized
the vibration of
a human voice so divine,
or plunged into
the shape of a human eye
before being hypnotized
by the blue on a screen?
We become
c o m a t i z e d
and we fade away
u n s e e n .

Inner Speech

When our words
are exhausted
and the world
dims its light,
we hear
that muffled voice
begin to narrate
the days of our lives.
We embark on
internal monologues
with this little voice inside,
simulating conversations
we had in the past,
or devising conversations
we have yet to have.
We conjure those we yearn
or those we mourn and begin to
s o l i l o q u i z e .

Transcendence

My moment of pure
transcendence
materializes
when the stars
inhabit the sky,
for that is when I realize
that I am nothing more
than a fading trace
against such
a vast design
unable to hold
or reach
the infinity
of something so divine.

Muse

The blood in
my veins
tinted with
a shade of pain
and a past that follows
close behind,
I find,
play the role
of being my muse
just as much
as the light
inside your eye.

Old Books

Dust collects
on top of old books,
the musky scent
of immortality
conquering time,
p r e s e r v i n g
what is no more
on fragile pages,
reminding us
of how we hope
to be preserved
in someone's
m e m o r y.

Live Fully

Life is short,
it will pass you by
in the blink of an eye.

Live then, and be
fully human,
loving fully.

Leave a mark
in time,
because,
when your gone,
all that is left
are the memories
you leave behind.

Fall

Fall into defeat
so you can rise
upon your feet,
reborn and resolved,
fully evolved.
Let strength
become your grace
and trace it as it
s o f t e n s
the glow in
your face.

Growth

Growth means
re-evaluating
hand-me-down ideals,
burning down
the ones that
do not fit our skin,
reducing them
to cinders in the air
gently grazing
at our hair.

Antiquity

Remember
those old ideals
that used to
navigate
your blood,
but remember them
at a distance.
Transform them
into will-o-wisps
flickering over
a marsh inside
your mind,
and be ready
to leave it all
b e h i n d .

It is this
distance
that allows us
to evolve.

Summit

When you reach
the summit
from challenges
s u r m o u n t e d ,
and you stand
on top of
the pile of selves
you bled
and all the skins
you shed,
take a breath,
look up at the sky,
and keep going.

                        There is no end
                        to your becoming.

Rise

I hold my sadness
in my palm,
my back wilts
as I sink
into cold sheets
that hold me tighter
than the grip I have
upon my dreams.
But I fight
and I will rise,
for my heart
still beats.

Stand

I may fall
time and time again,
and every time
I will always find
the morning bloom
of wildflowers
inside of me,
uncoiling bone
after bone
until my spine
forms
a straightened line.

I
will always
stand strong.

ABOUT THE AUTHOR

Barbara Garay is a writer and photographer based in Chicago, Illinois. Her poetry explores themes of loss, displacement, healing, trauma, pain, love, passion, introspection, and philosophy. Creative expression has always been a way to cope with early childhood trauma she experienced. She hopes her writing will also open a space for others to heal. She has been writing since childhood. She studied history and philosophy at Loyola University Chicago.

You can find Barbara Garay at:
www.facebook.com/writingsbybarbara and www.instagram.com/barbaragaraypoetry.

ABOUT THE BOOK

Beneath the surface is a collection of poetry about overcoming trauma, navigating love, enduring heartbreak, dealing with depression and anxiety, and coping by becoming emotionally resilient. The book is split into five chapters: Roots. Love. Heartbreak. Internal Struggles. Resilience.

www.ingramcontent.com/pod-product-compliance
Lightning Source LLC
Chambersburg PA
CBHW071404290426
44108CB00014B/1676